BRITAIN IN OLD PHOTOGRAPHS

THE NORFOLK BROADS

DAVID HOLMES

SUTTON PUBLISHING

Sutton Publishing Limited
Phoenix Mill · Thrupp · Stroud
Gloucestershire · GL5 2BU

First published 1996

British Library Cataloguing in Publication Data
A catalogue record for this book is available from the
British Library.

ISBN 0-7509-1277-4

Typeset in 10/12 Perpetua.
Typesetting and origination by
Sutton Publishing Limited.
Printed in Great Britain by
Ebenezer Baylis, Worcester.

Front cover: How Hill staithe, May 1913 – one of the Boardman twins tries his hand at fishing.
Title page: A wherry moored in Catfield Dyke, off Hickling Broad, c. 1900
Back cover: The front cover of Blake's 1946 Yachting List.

Horning village, c. 1899.

CONTENTS

The noted Norfolk naturalist Arthur H.
Patterson, photographed in 1923 as he left on
his little North Sea ketch, *The Walrus*, after
lunch with the Boardman family at How Hill.

A wherryman near the ice house at Catfield Dyke, off Hickling Broad, *c.* 1900.

INTRODUCTION

Four thousand years ago, Broadland was a wooded freshwater swamp. By Roman times, some two thousand years ago, the district was a shallow, muddy estuary, with tidal, salt-water conditions. More recently freshwater conditions returned. The next page of the geological history of the district has yet to be written, but the North Sea has a trick of regaining any territory previously surrendered. Much of Broadland regularly faces up to the threat of salt-water flooding, a risk which becomes more real with each passing winter. One day the Broads may again be a large, tidal estuary, a wild place for the birds, but with no place for swallow-tail butterflies, marsh orchids or water lilies.

The effect of these changes has been to lay down a kind of Victoria sandwich of alternating layers of peat, deposited in freshwater conditions, and clay, deposited in salt-water conditions. In medieval times, local residents discovered that the thick layer of brushwood peat, from four thousand years ago, while covered by other layers, provided an excellent source of fuel. In areas where the marine clay deposits were only a few inches thick, it was worthwhile digging through it to extract the peat. In other places the clay was too thick to be tackled by hand tools, so the brushwood peat lay untapped.

Water levels rose in the thirteenth and fourteenth centuries, sometimes with catastrophic results. At Hickling, according to the medieval chronicler, John Oxnead, 'nine score of different sexes and ages perished' in a major sea flood in 1287. In many parishes, the peat diggings gradually became seen in a new light – they filled with water and became valuable fisheries. For example, at the end of the thirteenth century South Fen in Martham was producing peat; by the end of the fourteenth century it was producing fish. A new way of life began to evolve, based on a variety of harvests of marsh crops, and enjoying a diverse wealth of natural sources of food. The arcane environment of the marshman, bringing up his large family in a waterside cottage, catching eels and wildfowl, was in tune with the harmony of the seasons. Judging by the very few written accounts of life in the marshes, it was a life apart from other men, and it would seem another world to us.

Thus the Broads are man-made, and have been described as the largest ancient monument in Britain. The rivers which link them into a navigable system are also very largely man-made. The natural shallow, winding channels have been widened, deepened, straightened and diverted, during a period of some hundreds of years, to produce today's familiar pattern. The rivers and Broads are fringed by marshes, which have been cut into and drained by ditches and which have been managed in a variety of ways. If nature had been allowed to take its course the marshes would all by now have become woodland or shallow expanses of open water. The rhythm of the seasonal marsh harvests has preserved reed beds and sedge beds, still producing crops for the thatcher. Sadly, the vast mowing meadows which produced sweet marsh hay for the work-horses of urban England have largely vanished. There are no longer any commercial osier beds, and more specialised marsh crops like the true bulrush are no longer harvested. Even the expanses of grazing marsh, home to splendid herds of dual purpose red poll cattle in Victorian times, have suffered neglect, or worse, been ploughed up altogether.

The population of the Broads area has always been exceptionally large for a rural district, and this helps in part to explain the huge volume of peat dug from the area. However, settlement is concentrated in a number of large villages, especially in the northern part of the Broads. These places have seen some dramatic changes, and the process of change continues still. Initially farming, peat digging, 'or turbary', and fishing were main activities, with a range of small-scale, cottage industries like weaving. Later, building the large, shallow draught boats of the Broads, especially wherries, became an important activity. Trading between the villages, and downstream to Yarmouth for coastal trade, or upstream to Norwich markets, rapidly became important. The presence of such an intricate pattern of waterways undoubtedly gave east Norfolk an early opportunity for development. The early stages of the Industrial Revolution contributed to a continuing pattern of prosperity – water transport and water power were concepts with which Broadsmen were quite familiar. Huge maltings grew up in many waterside villages in the early nineteenth century, and the malt trade ensured brisk traffic on the rivers for half a century. The new industrial brewers of the cities of England generated unprecedented employment and prosperity in such villages as Coltishall, Ludham and Ranworth. There were other trades too, which have long since vanished. As an example, a curious chalk-rich clay, marl, was extensively quarried upstream of Wroxham. The deep, steep-sided cuttings created a changed landscape, which became an early local attraction – known as 'Little Switzerland'; carrying this sticky, bulky commodity provided more work for wherries.

The navigable Broads waterways were extended upstream, to Aylsham in 1779, and to North Walsham in 1826. Locks had to be installed, and elsewhere grand plans were formulated to establish Norwich as a major port, using a canal, the New Cut, completed in 1832, as a link to the sea via Oulton Broad and Lake Lothing at Lowestoft. Although the waterways were transformed, their future was quickly blighted by a new, high speed form of transport. The railway came to Norwich in 1844, and it was soon clear that waterways would only be able to compete for a few of the traditional cargoes. The 'Canal Age' had given way to the 'Railway Age'. The coming of the railways, and the great Victorian invention of bank holidays, together with greater prosperity and increased leisure time for the middle classes all conspired to usher in the next great era for the Broads. A few articles appeared in London journals extolling the virtues of clean air, clean water, the joys of sailing, and the delights of nature, all to be found on the rivers of east Norfolk. Then, in 1876, G. Christopher Davies published his celebrated *The Swan and her Crew*, followed swiftly by *The Handbook to the Rivers and Broads of Norfolk and Suffolk*, succeeded in turn by no fewer than forty-nine more editions over four decades. Davies is thought of as a kind of 'inventor' of the Broads, but he was only one of many. The number of handbooks, guides, stories, logs of cruises, and so on, proliferated, and the Broads were opened up to all.

Initially dominated by sailing boats, the industry provided jobs for hundreds of boat builders and other skilled artisans. Individuals hired out craft, from wherries to rowing boats, and many founded firms which are still operating in the Broads today. An unusual pattern of marketing the holidays through third parties, in particular Blakes, from 1908, and Hoseasons, from 1944, acting as agents for the majority of boat-yards, is still in operation. The effect of all this activity on the traditional villages has been profound. Some of them still have charm, but none has the apparent appeal shown in many of the photographs in this book. The transformations of Hoveton and Wroxham over the past century, and the parallel changes in Potter Heigham, are quite breath-taking.

Marshy waterside places are always likely to attract wildlife, seen today as one more attraction of the Broads. In the past wild creatures were a resource to be harvested. It was quite possible to subsist on a diet of natural wild food, and in Victorian times it was equally possible to make – or at least supplement – one's living by shooting and capturing wild birds. Clearly wildlife was theatened on all sides – by nets and lines, by guns and by decoys – yet habitats in the wild places were still havens for numbers of birds that modern naturalists can only dream of.

Man created the Broads, and thousands of people have exploited them for a good living over the years. In this century it has often seemed that people have put such pressure on the Broads that they cannot possibly survive. However, the Broads can still offer a glimpse of their former splendour, and the pleasure which they provide to thousands confirms their position as one of Britain's best-loved holiday playgrounds.

Whether or not Christopher Davies discovered the Broads, he certainly started one continuing trend, that of producing Broads books. Hardly a sailing season has passed without its crop of new volumes, and, as a collector, I welcome each one. I am thrilled to put this book together, even though I know there will be criticism. However, I have tried to include more about the villages of Broadland, especially the bigger ones, which I trust makes this volume different to its venerable predecessors. I am aware that a small, but significant, part of Broadland lies in Suffolk, but, Norfolk born and bred, I feel unqualified to include this area. I leave it to others to record the undoubted treasures of Oulton Broad, Barnby, Beccles and Bungay.

There is something about the Broads which commands dedication and enthusiasm. Those affected, and I am one, love the Broads as they are now, as they will be in the future, and above all as they were in the past. There is only black-sailed wherry left, but most modern Broads souvenirs depict wherries, and the name wherry crops up in pub signs, locally brewed ale, and numerous local organisations. Enthusiasts, visitors and residents alike bathe in a kind of hazy nostalgia for the golden age of Broadland. This book is an attempt to prove that this view of the Broads is entirely justifiable, and I hope it gives much pleasure.

David Holmes
How Hill, Ludham.

Bob Smithson, noted Broadsman and gamekeeper, photographed at the Hickling Broad coot shoot of January 1951.

THE ANT VALLEY

Bringing in the marsh hay harvest at How Hill staithe, July 1904.

'The narrow Ant my venturers essayed
Thereafter to explore, all undismayed
By contrary winds; but as the needle's eye
Is hard for laden camels to pass by,
So is the tenuous Ant a stubborn stream
To sail, without the wind's abaft the beam.
Yet, after weary hours, to Barton Broad
They came at length. By now their precious hoard
Their store of golden days, was running low
"Tomorrow, back to Wroxham we must go . . ."'

Hugh Money-Coutts, The Broads, *1919.*

Wayford bridge, *c.* 1906. Shortly before this picture was taken an older humpback bridge had been removed – this view shows the 'new' bridge, in turn demolished to make way for a widened A149 in the late 1960s.

The Wayford Bridge Hotel, proprietor R.C. Couzens, *c.* 1910. This was just far enough from Norwich to make an interesting Sunday afternoon jaunt by coach. The photograph is called 'The Start for Home', perhaps after a bank holiday excursion. The hotel ceased trading in November 1961.

Stalham High Street, *c.* 1912. Stalham was always a green and leafy village, with lots of mature trees. The fire engine shed is just visible, left foreground, as is the Baptist church in the middle distance.

Stalham High Street, *c.* 1938. Many elements of this scene are still there, but the Railway Hotel was demolished to be replaced by the Grebe, set well back from the street; on the opposite side is the corn hall, built in 1855.

The Stalham fire, 1906. Hensman's Provision Stores and the local bank were destroyed in a fire on Guy Fawkes Night, 1906. The fire appliance, seen in this view, only had to be drawn from its base a little way down the street.

Stalham Green, *c*. 1914. Once separate from the 'town' of Stalham, and a slightly select area to live, the Green is now part of the ribbon of settlement which links Stalham Street with Sutton.

Stalham Brass Band, *c.* 1919. Originally founded in about 1880, this band is thought to be the oldest in East Anglia. In the middle of the group, legs crossed, is bandmaster Collison; the drummer is Lloyd Spanton; next to him, seated, is Gus Spanton. The current bandmaster, Gerry Thirst, has held the post for fifty years.

Troops marching through Stalham, *c.* 1915. The picture shows the 2nd Battalion of the 6th Sussex Regiment on parade during the First World War. Note the Sunday collars of many of the accompanying children.

Stalham school, *c*. 1914. The school was built in 1878, to provide elementary education up to the age of fourteen. Although it is now the town's first school, a new Central school was built next door in 1939, now Stalham High.

Stalham staithe, 1916. A staithe is a place where wherries load and unload. This view shows an officer on leave from the First World War – a blissful moment away from the torture of the trenches.

Stalham staithe, *c*. 1930. Stalham staithe served the village and several mills, so wherries were usually to be seen unloading coal and basic materials. Southgate Brothers' yacht station offered only a few yachts for hire at this time, as one of the smallest Broads fleets.

Cookes staithe, Stalham, from the river, *c*. 1929. The granary in the centre of this picture was built in 1808 over a closed dyke so that wherries could be pulled inside for ease of loading and unloading.

Stalham Staithe Mill, *c*. 1912. At this time, this corn mill was owned by Harry Burton, along with other businesses nearby. It was the first mill to be fitted with 'patent sails', replacing the traditional sailcloth and 'common sails'.

Bray's Farm, Sutton, *c*. 1900. The cart shed and the farm pond for watering horses create a tranquil scene representative of most farms in the district at this time.

Sutton staithe, *c.* 1914. Staithe and village had been separated from each other by the railway in 1879. The Staithe Hotel, opened in the early 1930s, also helped to change the scene — it achieved a high-quality reputation under its resident proprietor Basil Hitchin.

Sutton staithe, *c.* 1925. The *Reindeer*, from Southgate Brothers' yard at Stalham, could be hired for £6 per week in August. Note the wicker-covered stone bottle, much used for fresh water, sometimes harder to obtain than stronger beverages.

Neatishead Street, *c*. 1914. A peaceful scene, despite the curious animal stalking the street, which shows Duffield's butcher shop and the White Horse pub, offering Bullard's Norwich ales.

Barton Road, Neatishead, *c*. 1914. Another view of this quiet village, with the blacksmiths taking a moment to pose for the photographer.

Irstead church and staithe, *c.* 1900. This is a scene which is still recognisable today, although trees now obscure the view of St Michael's Church.

Maria on Barton Broad. Built in 1834, the *Maria* was owned by Sir Jacob Preston from 1837 till his death in 1894. Between 1837 and 1850 she was considered the fastest boat on the Broads; note her lateen rig and blunt bow.

Barton Regatta, 5 August 1929. The wherry race was a highlight of Barton Regatta, and this picture shows the wherry *Hilda*, coming in last on this occasion.

Barton Regatta, 1933. Another wherry race, this time only a few minutes after the start. The three wherries are the *Hilda, Lady Violet*, with white sail, and *Cornucopia*.

How Hill staithe, 1911. The Boardman family enjoy the gin-clear waters of the River Ant. Edward Thomas Boardman, architect and owner of How Hill, is seen sitting on the stern of an old eel catcher's houseboat. Swimming is suspended until the wherry has passed. The skeleton mill, an open trestle smock drainage mill which lifted water from the twenty-seven acres of grazing land known as Clayrack marshes, is also visible.

Marsh hay loading, How Hill staithe, August 1929. Sweet marsh hay gave fodder and forage for horses, and was a major crop in Broadland until the spread of motorised vehicles after the First World War.

Walter Woolston, gamekeeper at How Hill, 1912. A fine patriarchal figure, Woolston was a modest but knowledgeable countryman, who introduced the Boardman children to the ways of nature. He and his wife lived in the Mill House at How Hill, and looked after E.T. Boardman's estate in the early years of this century. The smock, a wonderful example of the craft, is still preserved.

Stuart Boardman, with horse-drawn reaper at work at How Hill Farm; Mr Bloom at the reins, August 1928. Stuart built up the fruit and holly business of the farm, but was killed in Malaya in 1942.

Walter Woolston punting on the River Ant, August 1912. The river was swollen, and the marshes flooded, after the six inches of rain which fell in twelve hours on Monday 26 August, a record for East Anglia.

Wherry *Hathor*, Neave's Mill, River Ant, August 1912. Woolston and his punt are actually on the marsh, with members of the Boardman family standing on the river-bank, shocked by the extent of this unique summer flood.

Wherries at Turf Fen Mill, How Hill, River Ant, 10 April 1930. A calm day, the *Stalham Trader* finding progress very hard, but the *Ella*, with her engine newly installed, making enviable progress southwards.

Wherry *Ella*, How Hill. The *Ella* photographed only moments before the previous picture; she was the last wherry ever built, 1911–12, and the first to be fitted with an engine, 1929. Her skipper was George Bates, whose brother, Bob, acted as mate.

Wherry *Stalham Trader*. Skipper David Scott is seen holding the main sheet, but his mate, known only by his nickname 'Duke', is propelling the wherry upstream by the traditional method of quanting. The long quant pole is pushed into the river bed, and firmly lodged against the shoulder: the operator trudges from bow to stern, and the vessel slowly moves forward. Long, calm days were a wherryman's nightmare, and the sight of the motorised Ella must have set 'Duke' thinking.

Wherry *Stalham Trader*. Another of this beautiful sequence, taken by Humphrey Boardman, immortalising the clear serenity of this April morning on the River Ant by How Hill.

Bittern at nest, How Hill, April 1926. Bitterns became very rare in the nineteenth century, but after strict protection they re-established themselves in the Broads in the early years of this century. Jim Vincent persuaded Humphrey Boardman to set up a hide, and Humphrey became the first person to photograph bitterns at the nest. The resultant series of photographs was published in *Country Life* in August and September 1926. The nest was, as always with bitterns, surrounded by water some six to eight inches deep, and was sited in a dense patch of reed-mace, close to the River Ant.

Humphrey Boardman, beside the bittern hide, 1926. The hide was positioned some fourteen feet from the nest. He took his photographs in, as Miss Emma Turner put it, 'the few days that a rowing man has at his disposal throughout the May term' (at Cambridge).

Old Ludham bridge, *c*. 1900. An inevitable constriction on the River Ant, the bridge survived the 1912 storm, but caused more extensive flooding upstream. It was, however, replaced by the County Council in 1915.

The wherry *Dispatch* at Ludham bridge, *c*. 1925. Ludham bridge was the centre of a small group of fine mills, and the one in the picture was just south of the bridge, on the east bank – it has been almost entirely dismantled. The *Dispatch* was owned by Harry Burton of Stalham Mill, and skippered by George Rump.

Ludham village centre and post office, *c.* 1908. Most of the buildings seen here are still there, but with the single exception of St Catherine's Church all have changed considerably, with new windows, new roofs, or general modernisation.

Dan England, Boardman's Mill, 1927. Ludham millwright Dan England built about thirty of these trestle smock mills, and is seen here, left, fitting a new turbine to lift water more effectively from the marshes to the River Ant.

THE THURNE VALLEY

'Quanting out of Horsey Mere, c. 1934.

'Gray landscape, silvered with a passing gleam
On stubble-field and fen, and distant shower,
And brown sails gliding on the sinuous stream
By meadow-scented banks, and silver bell
Floating across the flats, where Martham Tower
Stands on its hill, a lonely sentinel.'

G.F. Bradby, 'Silver Gray' (Horsey Mere, Sunday), 1904.

Peat digging, Calthorpe Broad, August 1920. While deep peat digging, which brought the Broads into existence, was no longer possible after *c*. 1450, there was a continuous tradition of shallow digging for this low grade fuel. The picture, one of a series taken by Robert Gurney, shows Mr Harmer carefully and arduously cutting out a substantial block of wet peat ready to be stacked to dry.

Calthorpe, 1920. Here the peat digging implement or 'becket' can be seen, together with a stack of freshly cut turves. This process created shallow turf ponds throughout Broadland, later colonised by marsh plants, especially saw sedge, used by thatchers for ridging and capping roofs.

The Footbridge
Waxham Water Mill

Lambridge Mill, Waxham Cut, *c.* 1927. It is still possible to navigate Waxham Cut in tiny boats, although this remarkable little bridge, which rolled out of the way to allow boats through, is long gone.

Bridge over Waxham Cut, *c.* 1900. This bridge has also gone, but it has been replaced. Very few craft reach this remote upper part of the Thurne system, which is north of Horsey Mere.

Horsey Mill, *c*. 1930. Perhaps the most famous of all Broadland drainage mills, built to lift excess water off the marshes, to enable grazing and harvest of marsh hay. Even the National Trust, its present owner, seems to find difficulty in describing these buildings, but they are mills whatever function they perform, and the often used term 'wind pump' is quite simply wrong; drainage mill or windmill is the correct technical description.

Cottages in Horsey, *c*. 1914. Horsey was always one of the remotest villages, sheltering in the lee of a line of low sand hills, and under threat of flooding from both sea and mere.

Horsey post office, *c.* 1920. On the lane towards the sea, this post office must have been one of the quietest in Broadland. In the same lane, slightly closer to the sea, is the celebrated Nelson Head pub.

Horsey sea breach, February 1938. After a night of gales, the sea broke through the sand hills and flooded 7,500 acres. Many had predicted the disaster, and indeed a breach had occurred before, most recently in December 1917.

The coast road, 1938. A gap of some 700 yards between Winterton and Horsey Gap, created by a storm surge on the night of 12 February 1938, was the main cause of the flooding.

The coast road, Somerton to Horsey, 1938. The sea flood was a great spectacle, and these photographs show how extensive the flooding was, as well as the turn out of spectators to view the scene.

The coast road, 1938. The flood waters continued to rise for some days, partly because of the open breach, and partly because of the effect of the tidal surge holding water back in the upper reaches of the Thurne.

Somerton staithe, 1938. These photographs serve to remind us of the fragility of the Broads, which face a renewed threat of salt-water flooding every winter; defences are better at Horsey now, but are weak at Sea Palling and Happisburgh.

Somerton, River Thurne, 1938. The dead horse which, curiously, forms the subject matter of this postcard view, was not the only casualty – an inevitable result of a surge of salt-water, which had a devastating effect on all the wildlife of the area.

Hickling staithe, 1938. The salt-water inundated Hickling village and Broad, killing tens of thousands of fish, and the Hickling fishermen caught some herring, smelts, and a grey mullet – small comfort for the loss of the best pike fishery in Britain.

Mending the breach, Horsey, 1938. The first two attempts were a complete failure, and a temporary closure was swept away. The breach was finally closed in April, and only in May did the waters finally recede.

Somerton staithe, c. 1919. The Somerton wherries were owned and operated by the formidable Thain family, headed for two generations by Dionysius Thain, senior and junior, a name inevitably shortened to Di by the other skippers.

Somerton staithe, *c.* 1920. Another view of the staithe, this time looking upstream. The water in the upper reaches of the Thurne was always exceptionally clean and clear, and this holds true even today.

Somerton village, *c.* 1930. Cars now park where the puddle used to collect, and the garage has gone, but the scene is still readily recognisable.

Martham ferry, *c*. 1909. This was really a floating bridge brought into position to cross to Heigham Holmes, north of the River Thurne. It has since been replaced by an even more remarkable ferry, hinged at the southern end to swing across the river.

Martham Green, *c*. 1920. The green at Martham is still the finest in the Broads. One of the two cottages in the middle of this photograph was later converted to a fish and chip shop, still flourishing.

Somerton Road, Martham, *c.* 1911. The cottages are still there, on a bend in the B1152 road. Broadland villages mostly seem to have been very leafy and tree-lined in former times; few are so today.

White Street, Martham, 1912. Six inches of rain fell on Monday 26 August, and the total for the twenty-four hours of the storm was 7.34 inches. The rain was accompanied by gale-force winds, which did much damage.

The bridge, Potter Heigham, *c*. 1914. Reputedly dating from 1385, but with many recent repairs and alterations, including an eighteenth-century brick parapet, this bridge helps to protect the Upper Thurne Broads from the worst excesses of modern tourism.

The Bridge Hotel, Potter Heigham, *c*. 1935. Built at the turn of the century, and always a hive of activity throughout the summer season, it was a sad day for Potter when this hotel was destroyed by fire in September 1990.

The Falgate Inn, Potter Heigham, *c.* 1904. An old-established inn which continues to flourish, despite a major fire on the night of 28 February 1994, and is still a popular hostelry on the main road towards Ludham.

Grapes' garage, Potter Heigham, *c.* 1924. Sidney Grapes, owner of this garage close to the River Thurne, was known throughout Norfolk as a comedian and raconteur. He is remembered for his 'Boy John' letters and his most enduring character, Aunt Agatha, a comic invention whose home-spun philosophy was greatly enjoyed by local audiences..

The staithe, Potter Heigham, *c.* 1908. All gone, in one of the saddest transformations of Broadland; this scene shows George Applegate's boatyard, the first in Potter Heigham, established in 1895.

Pipe laying, Potter Heigham, *c.* 1913. Putting services into Broadland was inevitably difficult, with marshes and rivers causing serious engineering problems. In this scene, a water main is being laid underneath the River Thurne.

Walter Woods, Potter Heigham, with Miss
Helena Nitch, April 1930. Walter's father, also
called Walter, had followed his father and
grandfather into boat-building, and had moved his
business to Potter Heigham in the twenties. In
1926 ill health forced him to hand over to his two
sons, Walter and Herbert, who were quite
different in temperament and character, but were
technically equal partners in the business.

Herbert Woods, Potter Heigham, c. 1949.
Having an unashamedly ambitious approach,
Herbert and his brother clashed on the future
of the business, and eventually he bought out
Walter's share of the business. The building in
the background is in fact a water tower,
cleverly disguised and still a well-loved Broads
landmark, built in the 1930s.

Peggy, River Thurne, *c.* 1930. *Peggy* and her
two sister yachts, *Joan* and *Mongoose*, were built
by George Applegate & Co. and were available
for hire at Potter Heigham. *Peggy* was twenty-
six feet long, and cost £7 10*s* for a week in the
high season, 1939 – £1 cheaper than the
advertised rate for the 1931 season.

Potter Heigham Regatta, *c.* 1911. The first Thursday in August was the traditional start of this popular
regatta, which was a great occasion, with sideshows, Underwood's fair, swimming races, the greasy pole,
and some serious dinghy races.

Potter Heigham railway station, *c.* 1900. The Midland and Great Northern Joint Railway linked the Broads with the urban east Midlands, bringing holiday traffic. The station opened in 1880 and was finally closed in 1959.

Post office, Potter Heigham, *c.* 1906. The old post office was just east of the railway line, and this picture was taken from the level crossing. The shop was owned by Mr Pollard, who also served as grocer and draper.

Duchess of Light, *c*. 1935. Herbert Woods' yard built high quality cruisers, and the 'Light' class were the most impressive boats of their day. *Duchess* is seen here outside the Willow Bungalow Hotel at Repps on the Thurne.

The White Hart, Repps, *c*. 1920. This little pub used to sell Broads souvenirs as well as ales. The building, now a private house, is still there, facing the main A149 Cromer to Yarmouth road.

Thurne staithe, *c*. 1948. Thurne village is still small and secluded, and these cottages remain. Hidden in the trees is the Lion Inn, converted from an old farmhouse into a hotel in 1935, and serving Lacon's Yarmouth Ales.

Thurne staithe, *c*. 1920. Even regular visitors to Thurne village will have difficulty in recognising this view, at the closed end of the Thurne dyke opposite the cottages.

Catfield Dyke, off Hickling Broad, c. 1930. Catfield was known for many years as 'Clever Catfield', perhaps because it had staithes on two rivers – this staithe leading to Hickling Broad and the River Thurne, and at least three staithes leading to Barton Broad or the River Ant. There was an ice house here, relic of the days when Broads ice was collected in the winter for the Yarmouth fishing industry.

Catfield Dyke, c. 1900. The wherry, stern-on making exact identification impossible, might well be the *Violet*, a well-known Catfield vessel. In front is an old reed lighter, used in the collection of marsh hay, sedge and reed.

Wood Street, Catfield, *c.* 1908. Catfield was a big village, with many separate hamlets, and Wood Street was one such, close to Barton Broad and served by its own staithe, Catfield Wood End staithe.

Stalham Road, Catfield, *c.* 1919. This was the main road through the village, and indeed it continued to carry the traffic from Cromer to Yarmouth until the closure of the railway in 1959 allowed the County Council to plan a new road.

The Pleasure Boat Inn, Hickling, *c.* 1906. One of the most famous of all Broadland pubs, the Pleasure Boat served wherrymen and villagers long before holiday makers appeared on the Broads.

The Pleasure Boat Inn, Hickling, *c.* 1930. The Pleasure Boat was extended at the turn of the century to give more accommodation for visitors. Even royalty has been known to frequent this inn, in the great days of shooting.

Post office and stores, Hickling, *c.* 1908. Mr Turner's general stores and post office in the main street at Hickling was only one of several thriving shops in this large village. It was later taken on by Mr Clifton, and has recently closed down.

Cottages, Stubb Road, Hickling, *c.* 1933. Many hundreds of small thatched cottages have disappeared over this century, too small for modern needs. Although the house at the extreme right is still there, all the tiny thatched cottages have gone.

Heath Priory stores, Staithe Road, Hickling, *c.* 1955. A much loved shop serving villagers and visitors alike, the thatched stores finally closed in the early 1970s, suffering from competition from a summer season store closer to the staithe.

Reed stacks, Hickling, *c.* 1923. The reed harvest starts after the first hard frosts, which strip off the leaves, and ends when the new shoots of reed, called colts, appear. In most years this means Christmas to Easter.

Weed-lifting, Hickling Broad, *c.* 1932. Hauling out weed from the main channels through this, the largest broad, was always a major task for the summer season; after a period of years when weed growth was minimal, or absent, it has recently been necessary to start a new regime of cutting.

Pleasure Island, Hickling Broad, *c.* 1908. Holding village fairs on islands was a tradition in both Barton and Hickling Broads; quite impossible today as the islands have suffered from serious erosion.

Hill Common, Hickling, *c.* 1912. The irony of East Anglian usage of 'hill' for anywhere slightly above water level is sometimes lost on outsiders; then as now, this track at the northern end of Hickling Broad gives superb views over the water.

Whiteslea Lodge, Hickling Broad, *c.* 1900. Whitesea Lodge was enlarged and thatched in 1931, to provide more substantial accommodation for Lord Desborough's shooting parties. Despite the improvements, it was still sometimes flooded in winter.

Hickling Broad coot shoot, 18 February 1927. This was a major event in the shooting calendar, held to control coot numbers seen as a threat to the breeding success of many species of duck. 1,175 coot were shot on this day.

Hickling Broad coot shoot, 9 February 1935. Only eleven guns were invited this time, as the numbers of coot on the Broad were lower. The leading punt is occupied by Lord Desborough's gamekeeper at Hickling, Jim Vincent.

Hickling Broad coot shoot, 31 January 1951.
The great age of shooting was already virtually
over, but the magic of the annual coot shoot
was still irresistible even to King George VI,
seen here talking to Colin MacLean who was
in charge of the shoot at this time. The King
had only a year to live. 961 coot were shot,
one of the last big bags, and one of the last
times that coot pie and coot soup were to be
served in the cottage kitchens of the village.

Hickling Broad coot shoot, January 1959. Socially these shoots brought together all types of people. The
picture shows the young Prince Charles in the foreground, who was brought to the shoot on this occasion
by his father.

Jim Vincent, Hickling, *c.* 1935. When Lord Lucas, Sir Edward Grey and Edwin Montagu took on the lease of the shoot at Hickling in 1909, they chose Jim Vincent as their keeper. Son of a local wildfowler, he became renowned as an expert in wildlife, fishing, and shooting, even enjoying an invitation to Sandringham from King George V in 1930. Lord Desborough, a famous all-round athlete, took over the shoot in 1926, and he gave full support to Vincent to run the shoot in his own way. Both Vincent and Desborough died in 1944.

Hickling Broad coot shoot, January 1951. The King is in the leading punt, with a worried detective squashed in behind him, and Hickling head keeper Ted Piggin has the privileged job of punting this unusual royal craft.

THE BURE VALLEY

The pleasure wherry Reindeer *moored by Horning Mill, just upstream of the Ferry Inn, c. 1921.*

'Ere dusk, Ted moored the ship by Horning Ferry;
They ate their meat; dim craft beyond the wherry
Beguiled the starry night with cheerful noise
And happy laughter; from astern, the boys
Cast loose the dinghy, clattering all the gear,
And lightly argued who should row, who steer,
Which way to set their course, upstream or down,
And where the ferry lay, and where the town.'

Hugh Money-Coutts, The Broads, *1919.*

Coltishall lock, *c.* 1905. A new navigation was opened in October 1779 to link Aylsham with the Broads system, which required locks here and at Buxton, Oxnead and Burgh, as well as Aylsham itself.

Anchor Street, Coltishall, *c.* 1920. Coltishall became a busy place in the 1850s, as huge maltings were built close to the river. Anchor Street had its share of these maltings but most closed during the First World War never to reopen.

Malthouse, or Rising Sun, staithe, Coltishall, *c.* 1919. The malthouse stand idle, and only a pleasure wherry waits at the staithe. Suddenly Coltishall is quiet after half a century of malting and milling activity.

Coltishall bridge, August 1912. Several houses were washed away, as well as the bridge, after the notorious summer storm. Coltishall was badly hit because Buxton lock, three miles upstream, gave way, causing a huge surge to hit the village.

Village centre, Coltishall, *c.* 1916. This view shows Roys' grocery and drapery in the middle distance, but at this time the shop in the foreground was used as the orderly room for troops billeted in the village.

Central garage, Coltishall, *c.* 1930. Sited within a triangle of roads, this garage used to provide the full range of services for the motorist. The unique breakdown truck was cut down from an Opel saloon car of the 1920s.

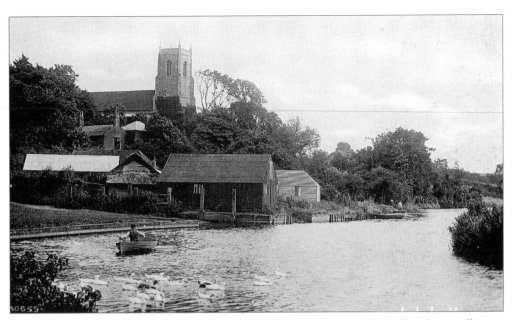

Belaugh, *c*. 1924. Somehow Belaugh managed to escape the many changes which affected most villages in the district, and the riverside scene, dominated by St Peter's Church, is still recognisable today.

Farming at Wroxham, *c*. 1920. This rural idyll is such a dramatic contrast to the modern scene that comment is scarcely necessary.

Roys' Stores, Hoveton, *c*. 1906. Arnold Roy followed his father's trade of shopkeeper, but he set up his own shops at Coltishall, Dereham and Hoveton. The site between the river and the railway station proved ideal, and the 'World's Largest Village Store' was born.

Stalham Road, Hoveton, *c*. 1920. The village rapidly became dominated by the growth of Roys', 'Universal Providers', giving a hint of things to come. Roys' service to boating parties, supplying everything they might need, and taking back anything unopened, proved highly profitable.

Hoveton village centre, *c.* 1948. Arnold Roy was joined by his elder brother Alfred, and they expanded the store rapidly – including the large grocery store opened in 1927, extreme right. By the way, newspapers should not be read in the street in Hoveton today.

Wroxham station, *c.* 1906. Porters and bookstall have long since gone, as have the posters advertising 'Half Price Season Tickets For Wives'. The station opened in 1874, although the line north to Cromer was not completed until 1877.

John Loynes, Wroxham, *c.* 1900. Acknowledged as the pioneer of the Broads hire boat industry, John Loynes moved his business from Elm Hill in Norwich to Wroxham Bridge in the 1880s. He was a remarkable entrepreneur and an expert boat builder; even before the First World War he was hiring out Norfolk-built yachts from Stavoren in Holland. He is reputed to have had a dislike of motor boats, but was astute enough to build them for hire to meet customer demands. John Loynes died in 1939, at the age of ninety-six.

Wroxham Bridge, *c.* 1914. This is the view from John Loynes' yard, looking towards the bridge and the two 'mills', as they were called, although one was a factory and the other a grain store. The industrial character of the area around the bridge has since given way to a sprawl of little shops.

Yacht *Coral*, Wroxham, *c*. 1908. One of John Loynes' cutter rigged yachts, the twenty-six ton *Coral* could be hired, with two attendants, for £16 per week in the high season of 1920.

Blossom, Wroxham, *c*. 1914. John Loynes can be seen in the stern of this ten-seater craft, built to take day trippers. His son, Robert, seen here at the wheel, skippered *Blossom* for much of her early life; another son, Jack, is also aboard, second from left.

H. Blake & Co.'s catalogue, 1908. Harry Blake's first list only included Ernest Collins' yachts. Blake's London-based marketing was so successful that most of the other yards quickly allowed their fleets to be offered in the same way.

Blake's Yachting List, 1913. By this time, some nineteen firms were included in Blake's list, but the hirer dealt easily and solely with Blake's, avoiding a variety of pitfalls and freeing the firms to concentrate on building and preparing their craft.

Norfolk Broads Holidays Afloat, 1946. This shows the cover of Blake's list in the first season after the Second World War. It was shorter and slimmer than the 1939 edition, since several boats were no longer suitable for hire after the war.

Norfolk Broads Holidays Afloat, 1949. The new format adopted in the late forties, and maintained through the fifties, reflected many changes in the industry. This list included only four wherry yachts – *Olive, Norada, White Moth, Rambler* – but offered a variety of small sailing boats for as little as £8 10s per week. Motor cruisers were in the ascendant, and by this time Herbert Wood's *Queen of Light* cost £47 10s per week in the high season. Two-berth motor cruisers, such as the *Peter Pan* class from Percivals of Horning, could be hired for £12 per week.

The Association, 1931. Although always referred to as 'Blake's', officially the boatyards had formed themselves into the Norfolk and Suffolk Broads Yacht Owners' Association. On the twenty-fifth anniversary of the Association they met at the King's Head Hotel, Wroxham, 7 December 1931. Top row, left to right: W. Hewitt, E. Southgate, G. Press, Clifford Smith, H.T. Percival, Herbert Woods, Percy Hunter, A. Fuller, C. Teader, Barney Broom, O.A. King, E.C. Landamore, W.S. Parker, Arthur Johnson. Middle row: Fred Press, George Hazell, W. Smith, H.C. Banham, Geoffrey Hart, Basil Broom, Percy Collins, Graham Bunn, A.G. Ward Hazell jnr, Martin E. Miller, Mr Barnwell, C. Mollett. Front row, sitting: J. Powles, H.J. Burrell, Dick Smallman, J.W. Eastwick, F. Miller, H. Blake, Leo A. Robinson, chairman, Mrs D. Blake, Alfred Pegg, C.H. Harris, R.W. Hawke, Mr Loynes.

View from Wroxham bridge, *c.* 1895. A pleasure wherry sails downstream into a scarcely recognisable rural landscape. Tied up are a trading wherry and, nearest the camera, a trader converted into a pleasure wherry; formerly the *Shepherd*, it has become the *Britannia*.

Changeover at Jack Powles' yard, Wroxham, 1946. The hire boat industry quickly got under way again after the war, and the rapid growth in ownership of private cars ensured that summer Saturdays would always be busy in Wroxham.

Norfolk Broads Yacht Club, Wroxham, *c*. 1938. The cover of this menu card provides glimpses of the stalwarts of the club. The club was formed in 1937, an amalgamation of smaller clubs, in order to take on a lease of Wroxham Broad. The four founder clubs were the Yare and Bure Sailing Club (founded 1907), the Great Yarmouth Yacht Club (1883), the Norfolk Dinghy Club (1931), and the Horning Town Sailing Club (1910), at that time proudly claiming the largest membership of any sailing club in the world, 571. In the middle of the montage, smiling but shown at an alarming angle, is Charles F. Carrodus, yachting correspondent for the *Eastern Daily Press*; top left is W.L. Clabburn, top right is Major Delaval Astley, and the couple peering from the tent are Dr and Mrs Tidcombe. Norfolk dinghies can be picked out as their sails carry the letter B.

Yacht *America*, Wroxham, *c*. 1900. Built by Ernest Collins, *America* was forty-three feet long and ten feet wide, and could be hired in August 1908 for £10 a week, complete with two attendants, although by 1920 the rate had increased to £15 10*s*.

Wroxham Week, 1952. This photograph recalls the annual team race between white boats, Yare and Bure One Designs, and brown boats, Broads One Designs. *Goshawk* (25), skipper Dr J.V. Morris, club commodore, and *Shearwater* (26), skipper Roger White, are seen overhauling *Azure Blue* (42), skipper John Habgood. This time the brown boats won.

Horning village street, *c.* 1908. The street at Horning runs parallel with the river, and inevitably shops sprang up to serve the needs of tourists. Much has changed, and many shops have closed, but the character remains.

Horning village street, *c.* 1930. Mr Sims stands at the door of his shop, which sold groceries, cakes and bread, together with all manner of other items, such as tobacco and post cards, but not milk — it was only a short walk to the dairy.

Horning village street, *c.* 1946. A similar view to the previous photograph, included to show how little change the war brought to this part of Horning. The motorcyclist is entranced by the fashions of the young ladies.

Town Reach, Horning, *c.* 1924. A lightly laden wherry sails down stream, passing a hire yacht. Town Reach was the main venue for Horning Town Regatta, started in 1903 by Edward Gillard, who also founded Horning Town Sailing Club.

Horning ferry, *c.* 1920. Many remember the small foot-ferry from Woodbastwick to Horning, but few recall that it was once large enough to take farm vehicles and cars. This ferry was destroyed by a bomb in 1941.

Horning Ferry Inn, *c.* 1929. The inn was destroyed by a German bomber on the night of 26 April 1941, just before closing time. Of fifteen bombs dropped, one destroyed the pontoon ferry, and another killed twenty-one people at the inn.

Horning Ferry Inn, August 1912. Another instance of the drama of the 1912 summer floods, this picture was taken from a rowing boat on the River Bure — the ground floor and bars are awash.

Horning Ferry Inn, August 1912. To the side of the Ferry Inn was a bowling green, but as this picture shows, play was interrupted for some days, while local lads enjoyed the new waterscape.

Turf-cutting implement, Horning, 1946. This becket is held by Mr Tom Garrod, who had described its use by his father to Charles Carrodus. Carrodus compiled two fascinating accounts of life in and around Horning, *The Horning Story* and *A Norfolk Village in Wartime*. He relates how the becket was used to cut turves measuring 3.5 inches in thickness and width, and up to three feet long. In the nineteenth century, cutting a thousand turves was said to be a good day's work, and the turf was taken by water to other parts of East Anglia. It was only a low grade fuel, and could not compete with coal once transport networks improved.

Robert Sims, Horning, *c.* 1946. Over ninety when the picture was taken, Mr Sims had always made his living on or near the river, and in the 1890s had operated an eel sett at Horning.

Salhouse village, *c.* 1904. Salhouse was untouched by the growth of the holiday industry. The village was well known as the centre of a high quality reed thatching business, that of Farman Brothers, the oldest thatching firm in England.

Salhouse Broad, *c.* 1922. Salhouse Broad always seemed peaceful by comparison with nearby Wroxham, and there was little evidence of the holiday industry. The farmer's wife at Broad Farm was apparently the only person to benefit, as she took in paying guests.

Salhouse Broad, *c.* 1913. Clearly this is a carefully posed picture, but nonetheless pleasing. C.R. Chamberlin noted that this Broad was called 'the Gem of Broadland', and gave its area as thirty-three acres in 1926. W.L. Rackham claimed that the view from the hills on the southern side of the Broad was 'the best view in Broadland' in 1927.

Salhouse Broad, *c.* 1905. A delightful scene; but the lilies represented a threat to Broads sailing, and some people were concerned that open water was about to disappear. Sewage and farm chemicals in later years ensured these fears were groundless.

Almshouses, Woodbastwick, *c.* 1906. Since most of the village has been owned by the Cator family for more than a century, it has been protected from development, and remains one of the quietest and prettiest in the district.

Cottages, Woodbastwick, *c.* 1924. These cottages facing the village green have recently been renovated and combined to form one dwelling, now called Evergreen Cottage.

The Maltsters, Ranworth, *c.* 1908. This is still one of the best-loved Broadland pubs, well situated opposite the staithe at Malthouse or Maltsters' Broad, and only a short stroll from St Helen's Church.

The Maltsters, Ranworth, *c.* 1947. The picture shows a happy gathering representing a variety of social classes, probably one of the many stops on a boating tour, this time sampling Steward and Patteson's Norfolk Ales.

Malthouse staithe, Ranworth, *c.* 1929. This gives a glimpse of those far off days when boats out-numbered cars at Ranworth. All is quiet, and no sails hoisted, so it is probably a Sunday morning, and most are at church.

Malthouse staithe, Ranworth, *c.* 1929. The two small lighters to the right of the picture were used to collect marsh hay, and the Broad looks crowded with craft, including two of the very latest motor cruisers built in the mid-1920s.

The wherry yacht *Goldfinch* at Ranworth, *c*. 1920. In the early years of the holiday trade, trading wherries were swept out and used for hire, then some were converted and some new pleasure wherries were built. But the wherry yacht gave hirers the opportunity to look rather smarter, to sit at leisure on a counter stern, and to have an altogether more civilised cruise. The *Goldfinch* could be hired for £23 10*s* a week, with two attendants, in the 1920 high season.

Marsh hay, Ranworth, *c*. 1914. Marsh hay was an important harvest of the marshes, and was brought back to the staithes by water. The lighters could be rowed from either end, and were shallow draught for use in marsh dykes.   -

THE LOWER BURE & THE TRINITY BROADS

St Benet's Abbey, c. 1918.

'. . . The green flats stretching far away
Where, yonder, like an ancient story,
St Benet's rises strange and gray,
The ghost of a departed glory.'

G.F. Bradby, 'St Benet's Abbey', 1904.

South Walsham street, *c.* 1909. The post office and general stores, also offering drapery, at that time kept by Mr E.B. Alexander, can be seen in the middle distance.

Cottages, South Walsham, *c.* 1912. These cottages, which still exist, were close to the Broad; the picture appears to capture a moment of social history, ladies of the vicarage or hall, perhaps, visiting the poor of the parish.

South Walsham staithe, *c.* 1919. Another load of marsh hay, freshly harvested, about to be unloaded on to the staithe. Marsh hay was a summer crop, and was never made into bundles, so it is easy to recognise in old photographs.

South Walsham staithe, *c.* 1920. This staithe was known as Jones's staithe, and was too narrow for yachts and cruisers to enter, although they could anchor in the Broad or tie up at Marjoram's staithe.

Marjoram's staithe, South Walsham, *c.* 1925. South from the River Bure along the Fleet Dyke, this staithe was at the entrance to South Walsham Broad.

Mrs Davey, Oby Mill, *c.* 1919. Mr Davey, mill-keeper and marshman, lived with his family in a bungalow at the foot of Oby Mill. Mrs Violet Davey tended the cows, pigs and poultry, and brought up her three children. The family's life was dominated by the wind, water levels, and the seasons on the marshes. Mrs Davey rowed to Upton or Acle, often with her bicycle on board, to collect supplies – she even cycled to Norwich, and still had to row the length of Upton Dyke at both ends of her shopping trip.

Part of Upton school, 1931. There were about seventy children in the village school at this time; now there is no school at all. Back row, left to right: Leila Lamb, Peter Jeffrey, Reggy Watling, John Curtis, Geoffrey Edrich, Edith Webster. Second row: Rita Curtis, Frances Chapman, Ruby Watts, Margery Willgress, Grace Curtis, Gertie Clare, Madelaine Smith. Third row: Madge Davey, Muriel Davey, Olive Mallett, Mrs Jeffrey and Nippy, Kathleen Jeffrey, Sylvia Watts, Amy Clark. Front row: Thomas Hammond, Harold Beck, Keith Watts. This picture was kindly loaned by Mrs Madge Ward, neé Davey.

Oby Mill, *c.* 1924. This four-storey mill bears the date of 1753 and is regarded as the oldest of the brick-built Broads drainage mills. The mill was on the Oby Manor estate of the Wiseman family, but Mr Davey acted as their marshman and looked after the mill from 1909 to 1939. In earlier times a saw bench was worked by the mill, in addition to its main work of drainage. In 1928–9 a diesel engine was installed, which Mr Davey always kept well polished. The mill was abandoned after the war, when Mr Percy Wiseman moved away from the district. It is still sometimes known as Wiseman's Mill. Mr Davey's son Herbert is seen in the rowing boat in this picture.

Lane at Upton, *c.* 1910. Upton has a small Broad, but this has never been navigable; the long dyke from the Bure enabled river craft to reach the village staithe.

Acle bridge, *c.* 1902. The finest of all the medieval bridges in the Broads, this was demolished in 1932. It was said to be haunted, hardly surprising as the bridge was used for several executions by hanging.

Haymaking, Acle, *c.* 1910. As in crofting areas today, all the family were recruited to help with the season's first harvest. Marsh hay grew so luxuriantly that there was always a second harvest later in summer, occasionally even a third cut.

Eel sett, *c*. 1900. No one seems entirely clear where this eel-catcher's hut was, but all are agreed on the magic of this picture, particularly the unique double bucket chimney.

Arthur Royce, eel-catcher, Acle, *c*. 1947. The eel net or sett is stretched across the entire river, traditionally at night, when the eel are on the move and boats are not. Here the business end of the funnel shaped net, the pod, is being inspected.

Eel-catcher, Acle, c. 1947. Here Arthur Royce is tipping part of the catch into an eel-trunk, a perforated wooden box which is lowered back into the water to keep the eels alive.

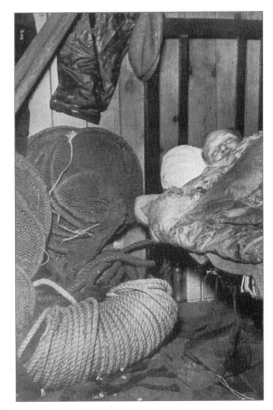

Inside Arthur Royce's eel hut, Acle, c. 1947. Clearly this is a posed shot, but fascinating enough. It gives a glimpse of a lost world – there is only one eel sett left, which is occasionally worked, but the catcher arrives by car and lives at a distance. The old eel men knew the ways of this curious fish, and knew its movements up and down stream long before scientists documented its unique transatlantic migration. They knew the exact combination of dark night, steady wind and rain, and ebb-tide, which brought the heaviest 'run' of eels.

Acle Regatta, *c.* 1911. In the late Victorian era, and the early years of this century, there were two wide stretches of river which attracted the bigger yachts. One was on the Yare at Cantley, and the other, shown here on Regatta Day, was upstream of Acle bridge.

Six Mile House Mill, Halvergate, *c.* 1920. The open grazing marshland between Acle and Great Yarmouth is still noted for its unique array of drainage windmills, but many are now derelict and few have sails. This mill, also known as Lake's Mill, is now in ruins. It is about 1½ miles downstream from the restored Stracey Arms Mill, on the south side of the Bure. Typical of the tower mills in this area, this example has four storeys, is brick built, but tarred, and has an eight-bladed fantail.

Ashtree Farm Mill, *c.* 1949. The old boatmen of Yarmouth called the River Bure the 'North River', and this mill was their first south bank landmark sailing northwards from Yarmouth. There has been a mill on this site for much more than a century, but the present structure dates from 1912. It was still working until it was extensively damaged in the storm and flood of 31 January 1953. This means that Ashtree Farm was the last Broadland drainage mill to be built, and the last to be worked regularly. It has now lost its cap and sails, and is derelict, but the Norfolk Mills and Pumps Trust has plans to restore it.

Stokesby, *c.* 1931. Yachting parties coming upstream from Yarmouth were intended to notice Mr Osborne's Provision Stores sign, prominently displayed on the gable, and tie up at the quay. The remains of a corn windmill, built in 1826, can be seen behind the stores.

Stokesby, *c.* 1925. The Methodist chapel, centre right in this view, was built in 1811 but was sold as a private house in 1927. Later it became the village hall, and was demolished in 1986.

Billy Tooley, wherryman, *c.* 1929. As Roy Clark puts it, 'independent admirably describes Billy Tooley'. He was owner and skipper of the *Widgeon*, and he only reputedly took a cargo if it suited him and his immediate plans. The *Widgeon* was a twenty-eight ton wherry built at Wroxham in 1897; she was fire-bombed on Breydon at the beginning of the Second World War, and Billy Tooley perished with her.

The *Luna*, Runham Swim, 1952. The *Luna* was built for Horace Bolingbroke in 1902 and he sailed her until 1921. She was owned by J.M. Platt from 1951 to 1965. Mr Platt, who loaned this photograph, bought her for £150 at Wroxham boat sale, after the auctioneer had mistakenly omitted to put her up for sale and was obliged to offer her at the reserve price.

Ormesby Broad, *c.* 1912. The Trinity Broads, as Wentworth Day called them, are quite different in character to the rest of the system. Although connected to the Bure by means of the Muck Fleet, this has never been navigable, so there were no staithes, no wherries, and no hire craft other than dinghies. Even the names of the Broads present difficulty – the northernmost is definitely Ormesby, and the southernmost is Filby, but in between are Lily Broad, Rollesby Broad, and, on some maps, another Ormesby Broad.

The Eel's Foot Inn landing stage, Ormesby St Michael, *c.* 1912. Still one of the best places for coarse fishing in Broadland, the Eel's Foot developed as a popular resort for an evening or afternoon drive from Yarmouth.

The Sportsman's Arms landing stage, Ormesby, *c.* 1908. Once rivalling the Eel's Foot as a hostelry and as a fishing spot, the Sportsman has long since closed. The building is still there, opposite the garden centre, but few would realise it was ever a pub.

Ormesby Broad, *c.* 1954. Still one of the purest of all the Broads, Ormesby has long provided water for the Yarmouth area. The East Anglian Water Co. was a private water firm years before the general privatisation of water supplies.

The blacksmith's shop, Rollesby, *c.* 1908. All the villages had smithies, providing a range of services; this one undertook a good deal of work on wagons and carts. The buildings have gone from this site, which was on the north side of the main road.

Osier harvest, Filby, *c.* 1919. The five main marshland crops – hay, reeds, sedge, rushes and osiers – were represented in all the larger parishes. Baskets are still made in Yarmouth, but the osier beds have all become derelict, and imported willow is used.

Filby bridge, *c.* 1910. The A1064 road uses the isthmus of land between Filby and Rollesby Broads, just as the A149 uses the strip of land between Rollesby and Ormesby Broads. These tongues of land were left by the original peat diggers centuries ago.

Reed-cutter, Filby, *c.* 1900. The reed bunches are tied with baler twine today, but in the past the reed-cutter would use a twist of vegetation to secure the bundle – a forgotten art.

THE SOUTHERN RIVERS

The grandest structure of the entire Midland and Great Northern Joint Railway, the viaduct over Breydon
Water, was completed in 1903 and dismantled in 1962.

'On Breydon Water, when the tide is out,
The channel bounds no sailorman can doubt
Starboard and port, the miry banks reveal
Where safety lies beneath his cautious keel.
But when the flood has wiped the water clean,
– Hiding the muddy haunts where seagulls preen
Their wings, and shake their heads – black pillars mark
The channel's edge for each adventuring bark.
Beware; the channel shifts, and now and then
A post deceives the hapless wherrymen.'

Hugh Money-Coutts, The Broads, 1919.

The Monkey House, Whitlingham, *c.* 1905. This curious building stood opposite the Thorpe Asylum, across the River Yare, until it was removed and re-erected near the M and GN railway station in Norwich.

Postwick Reach, *c.* 1919. The Yare, being wide and deep, often provided easier going for wherries, and cargoes on the 'Norwich River' were not hard to come by. This wherryman has fitted the 'bonnet' to his sail, an extra yard of sail for use in light winds.

Bramerton, *c*. 1912. In the distance is the Wood's End, then a hotel and popular destination for steam boats from Yarmouth and Norwich. In the 1930s, a daily river service, throughout the summer, brought trippers from Norwich for afternoon tea.

Reed-cutting, Surlingham, February 1953. From right to left, the picture shows Mr Sharman, Russell Sewell, and Ted Ellis. Probably the greatest naturalist Norfolk has ever produced, and the acknowledged expert on the Broads, Ted was respected and loved by all.

Surlingham ferry, *c*. 1924. The River Yare had no road bridge between Carrow and Great Yarmouth until the Norwich southern bypass was built, but although Reedham ferry still operates, all the other chain and windlass ferries have now gone. The Ferry House is still thriving, but no longer serves Youngs and Crawshay's Champion Norwich Ales.

Surlingham Ferry Inn and staithe, *c*. 1901. Wherry trade linked all the riverside villages, and all the necessary bulk commodities were brought in by water. Here the task of unloading coal from the wherry *Meteor* is almost complete. The ferry last operated in 1943–4.

Coldham Hall Hotel, *c.* 1912. The proprietor of the inn was Albert Godwin, and he is shown here flanked on either side by two of his bar staff. By 1936, the inn had passed to Mr W.J. Breach, but still served Morgan's Ales.

Coldham Hall, *c.* 1915. This rowing boat served for many years as a passenger ferry from Brundall to Coldham Hall, and the steam drifters were apparently tied up here, where the river was wide, before being broken up for scrap in Norwich, a sad ending.

Carting marsh hay, Rockland St Mary, 1912. Since the regular marsh hay harvesting ceased, the entire Broads landscape has changed; marshes quickly turn into scrubby woodland when they are not cut, and the open character of the fens is lost.

'Scientific' Fuller, Rockland, c. 1913. Jimmy Fuller, described by William Dutt in 1903 as 'one of the few men who manage to gain a livelihood much after the fashion of the old-time Broadsmen', spent more than sixty years on or around Rockland Broad, especially aboard his beloved gun punt.

Loading reeds, Rockland staithe, *c.* 1956. The picture shows Mr Alfred Stone of Rockland St Mary loading some very high-quality bundles of reed. Mr Stone was known in the village as 'Fudgie', and was always busy. In spring and summer he looked after his market garden, producing vegetables for local markets, but in the winter the reed harvest dominated his time.

Reed-cutting, Rockland; *c.* 1956. 'Fudgie' Stone has help here from his son Brian – note that short handled sickles are used for the harvest, unlike the curved scythes familiar in many reed beds today.

Brundall Reach, *c.* 1938. Brundall had the advantages of proximity to Norwich and an excellent rail service. In the 1930s, James Hobrough & Son developed a bungalow estate between the station and the River Yare, for sale and for holiday lets.

Brundall Gardens, *c.* 1930. The gardens, including a 7½ acre lake, were created between 1892 and 1908 by Dr Michael Beverley. In 1920 they were opened to the public on a regular basis, with a landing stage for Yarmouth steamers and a large refreshment room.

Boatbuilding at Brooms, Brundall, *c.* 1949. The firm of C.J. Broom and Sons, established at the turn of the century, achieved an enviable reputation for quality, and during the Second World War constructed almost 500 craft for the Admiralty. In the 1950s and '60s most Broads boatyards went over to the new glass fibre methods of construction.

Cantley sugar factory, 1912. Although the Dutch had persuaded some Norfolk farmers to grow sugar beet before this date, the Cantley factory was the first to be built in the UK. It was opened in November 1912 and employed nearly 500 men.

Dutch workers, Cantley, 1912. The firm which developed the Cantley factory, the Anglo-Netherlands Sugar Corporation, naturally brought in some Dutch workers to pass on the necessary skills to the local workforce.

Cantley sugar factory, c. 1924. The factory was sited by the river so that sugar beet, a bulky commodity, could be brought in by wherry. The factory was closed in 1916, reopened in 1920, and accepted its last water-borne delivery of beet in 1951.

Langley Mill Marshes, 1953. On the night of Saturday 31 January, a ferocious northerly gale whipped up the highest tide ever recorded in the North Sea, subjecting the entire east coast to a catastrophic surge. The photograph shows one of the hundreds of breaches which occurred in the river banks of Broadland. In Norfolk as a whole, 26,000 acres of farmland were submerged, and ninety-eight people died.

Hardley Clay Pits, June 1914. J.S. Hobrough's, a remarkable firm with interests in wherries, dredging, engineering and building, dug clay at Hardley for brickmaking. The scene is uncannily like one's imagined view of a medieval peat digging.

Pye's Mill, Loddon, *c.* 1900. Once within sight of the River Chet and the Church Plain in Loddon, there are now no traces of this superb post mill. The mill had a brick-built roundhouse, and above this the post mill revolved so that the sails faced into the wind. Turning to wind was achieved by the eight-bladed fantail, which rested on wheels on the ground, and was attached to the rear door of the mill by means of an access ladder with supporting struts. Note the corn shocks, or stooks, in the foreground; sheaves of corn stood up in a tent-shape to dry the crop.

Blacksmiths, Loddon, *c.* 1914. The smithy was next to the Fox & Hounds Inn. Mr Bertie Fisk, master blacksmith, is seen standing (in the group of four with arms folded, he is second from right) together with his apprentices, staff, and officers billeted locally.

Great Eastern Railway bus, Loddon Church Plain, *c.* 1910. The railway never came to Loddon but the GER Company provided an omnibus service between Norwich and Beccles. The conductor of this vehicle, Arthur Smith, was killed in action in the First World War.

Loddon Water Mill, *c.* 1920. Norfolk, despite its slow rivers, had 500 water mills at the time of Domesday, but by 1890 only a handful remained. Loddon mill was actually converted to steam in 1888, and continued working for Woods, Sadd and Moore until the 1960s.

Loddon staithe, *c.* 1925. The narrow River Chet provided a link for Loddon with the River Yare, but as the next picture shows, the Chet is really a canal; previously wherries unloaded at Langley or Hardley staithes and cargoes were carried to Loddon by road.

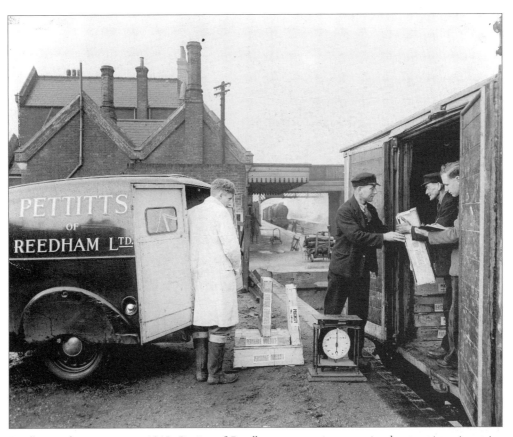

Reedham railway station, *c.* 1945. Pettitts of Reedham was a quite exceptional enterprise, pioneering frozen food technology and providing a market for a huge network of small poultry and rabbit breeders across Norfolk. The station was always ready to ship out the next consignment.

Unloading cockerels, Reedham, *c.* 1945. The picture shows Lou Edwards, driver and collector for Pettitts, with Kathleen Cross. The rounds for poultry, game and rabbit collection were worked out with military precision, and covered most of Norfolk and north Suffolk.

Pettitts, Reedham, *c.* 1944. Founded in 1922, by Mr V.C. Pettitt, this was an imaginative family business, based on the concept of finding a use for everything – even fur and feathers were used to make items of great beauty for sale and exhibition. These ducks are being fed on 'Tottenham Pudding', which was 100 per cent household waste from Norwich, supplied and processed by Norwich Corporation during wartime.

Reedham church with girls from Pettitts, *c.* 1940. During the war the operation at Pettitts increasingly depended on female workers, including, left to right: Phyllis Mallett, Hazel Edwards, Daphne Mallett, and Kathleen Cross.

The Eagle, Reedham, *c.* 1946. There is still one pub in the square beside Reedham station, the Railway Tavern, but the Eagle Tavern closed in 1961. The picture shows Stanley and Jessie Carter, who ran the Eagle from 1938 to 1951.

Reedham ferry, *c.* 1951. This, the last chain ferry in Norfolk, still operates. This particular pontoon was built in 1914, refurbished several times, and was transformed by the addition of an eight hp engine, instead of the hand crank, in 1950. It was retired in 1983, when a new pontoon came into service.

Charlie Stone, Reedham, *c.* 1935. Charlie Stone was licensee of the Reedham Ferry Inn from 1917 to 1941; this photograph was kindly loaned by the current landlord, Mr David Archer.

Reedham Ferry Inn, *c.* 1938. This famous and popular Broadland pub has been enlarged and substantially altered to provide large bars and restaurant accommodation. The picture shows the inn before any of these changes had been planned.

Geldeston lock, *c*. 1907. The Waveney Navigation between Bungay and Beccles had three locks, at Wainford, Ellingham, and Geldeston, also known as Shipmeadow lock. The navigation was closed in 1934 and the locks fell into disrepair.

The *Bramble* on the Waveney, *c*. 1924. This view of a pleasure wherry became famous as part of an advertisement for LNER, promoting cheaply priced return tickets to ten Broadland railway stations. The *Bramble* offered every facility for a luxurious cruise – piano, electric light, hot water in each cabin, a full-size bath, and a Thornycroft diesel engine.

The braiding room, Waveney Rush Growers, Aldeby, *c.* 1958. Originally this industry was started to provide work at Waveney Apple Growers outside the fruit packing season – it still flourishes at Aldeby. The picture shows the girls braiding the rushes into strips which are stitched together to make a variety of mats and baskets. The girl nearest the camera is Margaret Sharman.

The mangle, Waveney Rush Growers. Local rushes were used, seen stacked on the right, and they had to be flattened; in this picture the mangle is being turned by Joy Jenner, while Joyce Spall feeds the bolt of rushes through.

Waveney Hotel, Burgh St Peter, *c.* 1907. From 1904 to 1914, Frank E. Rice FZS ran a zoo at this site, now the Waveney River Centre. On the wall is the legend 'To The Bears', but in 1907, two healthy brown bears were shot, in public, to provide steaks for the villagers.

SS *Resolute*, on Breydon Water, *c.* 1958. One of many steamers to take trippers up river from Yarmouth, the *Resolute*, built in 1903, was taken out of service in 1963. Later hopes of a restoration were dashed by shortage of funds, and she was abandoned in 1979.

ACKNOWLEDGEMENTS

The majority of the photographs came from my own collection, built up over twenty-five years. However, it is a great pleasure to record my thanks to the many generous people who have lent precious pictures, or have helped with information: Terry Abbott, David Archer, Mike Barnes, Humphrey and Isobel Boardman, Michael and Pauline Boardman, Hazel and Len Funnell, Marion Green, Michael Gunton, Marie Hartley, Ann Hollis, Trevor Kay, Ruth Knight, Murial Loynes, Sydney Loynes, Robert Malster, Joan Morton (née Morris), Simon Partridge, Roger Peverett, Shirley Place, John Platt, Colin Prentice, Bryan Read, Nicholas Reynolds, Michael Seago, Richard Seago, Richard Shepherd, Daisy Stone, Jonathon Stone, Gerry Thirst, Jess Tunstall, Madge Ward (née Davey), Heather Wright. I would also like to thank Blake'0 s Holidays Ltd, Broads Tours Ltd, *Country Life* Magazine, Pettitts Animal Adventure Park, Waveney Apple Growers.

I must also thank all those kind people who offered me material which, for one reason or another, I was unable to use this time.

I have been unable to trace copyright holders in one or two cases. In particular, three pictures have been taken from a book by Charles F. Carrodus, *Life In A Norfolk Village, The Horning Story*, Norwich, 1949. These photographs were taken by Horace Grant, and the book was published by the late-lamented Soman-Wherry Press.

The verses which introduce each section were taken from *Broadland and Other Poems*, by G.F. Bradby, published by Elkin Mathews, London, 1904, and from *The Broads—1919*, by Hugh Money-Coutts, published by John Lane, The Bodley Head, London, 1920. This latter was an account, in verse, of one of the first pleasure cruises after the Broads were reopened following the Great War — even so the cruise was hampered by sunken craft at Hickling and Horsey, deliberately positioned to hinder an invading enemy.

I must also record my thanks to colleagues at How Hill for their forbearance when my thoughts have been focused on the Broads fifty years ago instead of the Broads here and now, and of course my wife Sue for help, support, and the most accurate rapid typing I have ever known.

I have tried to provide meaningful information with each picture, but sometimes this relies on memory, a treacherous source. Let me know if you find errors.

David Holmes
How Hill, Ludham.